Learn to Draw
UNDERWATER LIFE

www.av2books.com

AV² provides enriched content that supplements and complements this book. Weigl's AV² books strive to create inspired learning and engage young minds in a total learning experience.

Your AV² Media Enhanced books come alive with...

Audio
Listen to sections of the book read aloud.

Key Words
Study vocabulary, and complete a matching word activity.

Video
Watch informative video clips.

Quizzes
Test your knowledge.

Embedded Weblinks
Gain additional information for research.

Slide Show
View images and captions, and prepare a presentation.

Try This!
Complete activities and hands-on experiments.

... and much, much more!

Go to **www.av2books.com,** and enter this book's unique code.

BOOK CODE

N 8 1 9 8 1 1

AV² by Weigl brings you media enhanced books that support active learning.

Published by AV² by Weigl
350 5th Avenue, 59th Floor
New York, NY 10118
Website: www.weigl.com   www.av2books.com

Library of Congress Cataloging-in-Publication Data

Underwater life / edited by Heather Kissock.
     pages cm -- (Learn to draw)
ISBN 978-1-61913-240-5 (hardcover : alk. paper) -- ISBN 978-1-61913-245-0
(softcover : alk. paper)
1. Marine animals in art--Juvenile literature. 2.
Drawing--Technique--Juvenile literature. I. Kissock, Heather.
NC781.U53 2012
743.6--dc23
                         2012000468

Printed in the United States of America in North Mankato, Minnesota
1 2 3 4 5 6 7 8 9 0   16 15 14 13 12

042012
WEP050412

Senior Editor: Heather Kissock
Art Director: Terry Paulhus

Contents

6

10

14

18

22

26

Why Draw?

Drawing is easier than you think. Look around you. The world is made of shapes and lines. By combining simple shapes and lines, anything can be drawn. An orange is just a circle with a few details added. A flower can be a circle with ovals drawn around it. An ice cream cone can be a triangle topped with a circle. Most anything, no matter how complicated, can be broken down into simple shapes.

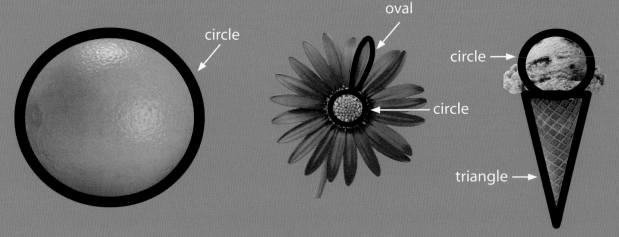

circle

oval

circle

circle

triangle

Drawing helps people make sense of the world. It is a way to reduce an object to its simplest form, say our most personal feelings and thoughts, or show others objects from our **imagination**. Drawing an object can help you learn how it fits together and works.

What shapes do you see in this car?

It is fun to put the world onto a page, but it is also a good way to learn. Learning to draw even simple objects introduces the skills needed to fully express oneself visually. Drawing is an excellent form of **communication** and improves people's imagination.

Practice drawing your favorite underwater animals in this book to learn the basic skills necessary to draw. You can use those skills to create your own drawings.

Underwater Life

People have been fascinated by underwater life for centuries. Many types of animals live underwater. Some live in rivers, lakes, or ponds. Others live in oceans. Underwater animals have **adapted** to moving and breathing in watery habitats. They have also adapted to avoid predators.

Each underwater species has its own special features. Drawing the underwater creatures in this book is a great way to learn about the different parts and features that make these animals successful in their environment. As you draw each animal in this book, think about how it uses its body to survive.

Meet the Crab

A crab wears its bones on the outside of its body in the form of a shell. This is why crabs are considered a type of shellfish. There are about 10,000 kinds of crab in the world. Crabs live both on land and in water.

Crabs come in a variety of sizes. The pea crab is only 0.75 inches (2 centimeters) wide. The Japanese spider crab is the world's largest type of crab. It can have a leg span up to 12 feet (3.7 meters) wide.

Eyes

A crab's eyes stick out from its head. They are located on long, thin tubes called stalks. Crabs can raise or lower the stalks. This helps them see objects around them without having to turn their body. Crabs can turn their eyes to see in different directions.

Legs

Crabs have 10 legs. Two of these legs are claws. Crabs often walk sideways.

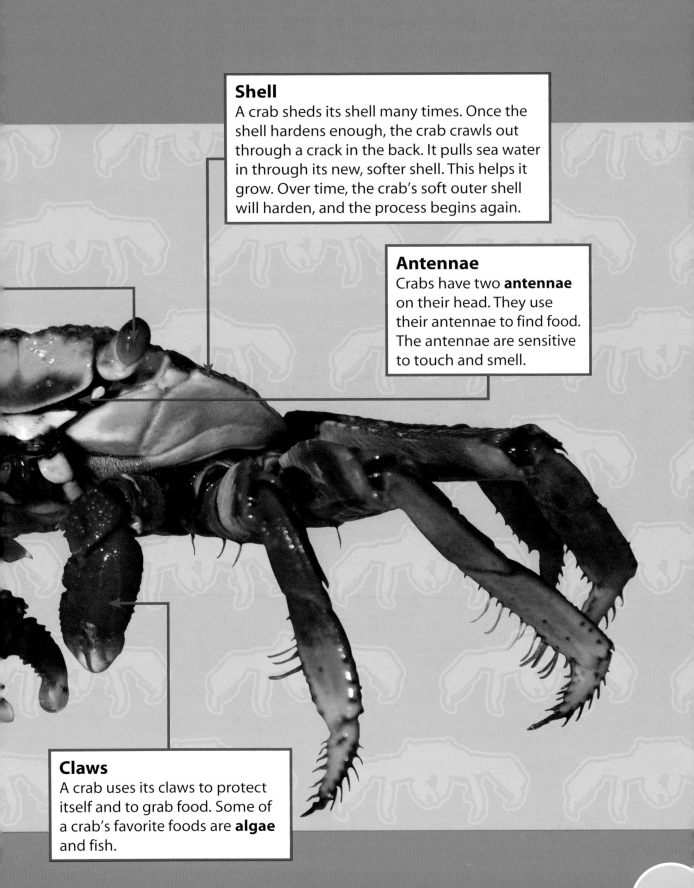

Shell
A crab sheds its shell many times. Once the shell hardens enough, the crab crawls out through a crack in the back. It pulls sea water in through its new, softer shell. This helps it grow. Over time, the crab's soft outer shell will harden, and the process begins again.

Antennae
Crabs have two **antennae** on their head. They use their antennae to find food. The antennae are sensitive to touch and smell.

Claws
A crab uses its claws to protect itself and to grab food. Some of a crab's favorite foods are **algae** and fish.

How to Draw a Crab

1 Start with a simple stick figure of the crab. Use a large oval for the body and curved lines for the legs and claws.

2 Draw the shell.

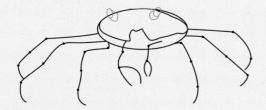

3 Next, draw the eyes.

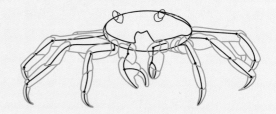

4 In this step, draw the legs and claws.

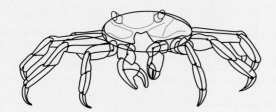

5 Next, draw the details on the shell.

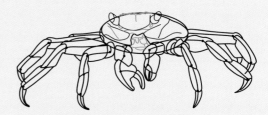

6 Now, draw the abdomen.

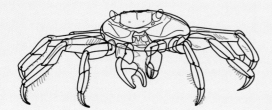

7 Add details to the legs, claws, and shell, as shown.

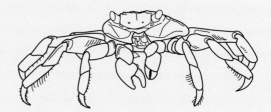

8 Erase the extra lines and the stick figure frame.

9 Color the image.

Meet the Jellyfish

Jellyfish are a kind of ocean animal, but they are not fish. Jellyfish are jiggly like jello. This is because they have jelly inside their bodies. There may be more than 2,000 kinds of jellyfish. About 200 have been described by scientists.

Jellyfish make their homes in oceans all over the world. They live in cold arctic waters and warm tropical waters. Jellyfish can be found near the shore and in the darkest, deepest parts of the ocean. There is even a type of jellyfish that lives in lakes and ponds.

Bell

Many jellyfish are shaped like an open umbrella. The part of the jellyfish that looks like the top of an umbrella is called the bell. The mouth and stomach of the jellyfish are found inside the bell. The bell is covered in a thin skin and is filled with a type of jelly.

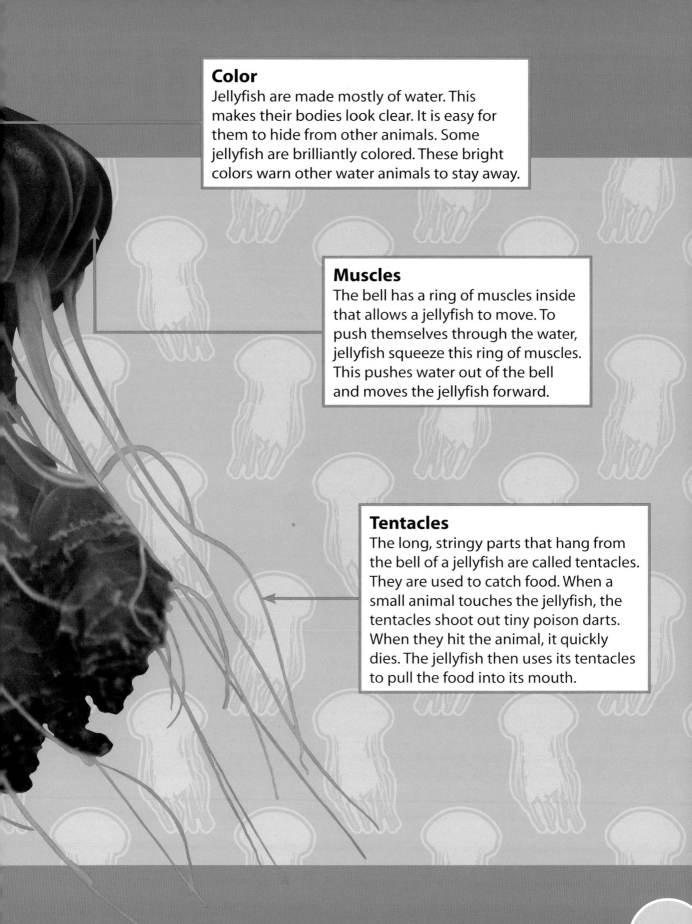

Color
Jellyfish are made mostly of water. This makes their bodies look clear. It is easy for them to hide from other animals. Some jellyfish are brilliantly colored. These bright colors warn other water animals to stay away.

Muscles
The bell has a ring of muscles inside that allows a jellyfish to move. To push themselves through the water, jellyfish squeeze this ring of muscles. This pushes water out of the bell and moves the jellyfish forward.

Tentacles
The long, stringy parts that hang from the bell of a jellyfish are called tentacles. They are used to catch food. When a small animal touches the jellyfish, the tentacles shoot out tiny poison darts. When they hit the animal, it quickly dies. The jellyfish then uses its tentacles to pull the food into its mouth.

How to Draw a Jellyfish

1 First, draw a stick figure of the jellyfish, as shown.

2 Now, draw the bell.

3 Next, draw the muscles on the bell.

4 In this step, draw large, inner tentacles.

5 Next, draw the outer tentacles.

6 Add details to the inner tentacles.

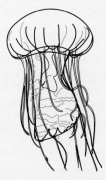

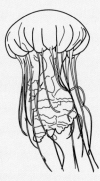

7 Draw small curved lines on the inner tentacles and bell, as shown.

8 Erase the extra lines.

9 Color the image.

Meet the Manta Ray

A manta ray is a sea animal that looks like a floating cape. Manta rays have very flat, wide bodies. The fins on their sides look like wings. This gives them a diamond shape.

Manta rays can be huge animals. Some adults are more than 23 feet (7 m) wide. This is the size of a small plane. The largest manta ray ever seen was 30 feet (9 m) wide.

Head
A manta ray uses two long lobes on its head to catch its food. These lobes act like funnels. They scoop water and food into the manta ray's mouth.

Slime
Manta rays have a thick layer of slime on their skin to protect it from germs.

Color

Each manta ray has its own pattern of colors. On their backs, manta rays are black, gray, or blue. This helps them blend in with the water. Manta rays are white or gray on the bottom. This helps them blend in with the sky when viewed from below.

Fins

The manta ray uses its two sets of fins to move through the water. It also uses them to jump out of the water. Some manta rays have even been viewed doing somersaults in the air.

Gills

A manta ray has gills on either side of its head. Water enters the ray's mouth and passes over its gills, allowing it to breathe. The gills also have a special part that strains food from the water and pushes it toward the ray's throat.

How to Draw a Manta Ray

1 Make a stick figure frame of the manta ray. Draw an oval for the body and lines for the fins.

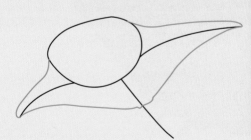

2 Draw the fins.

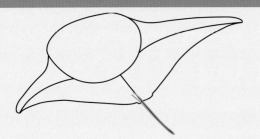

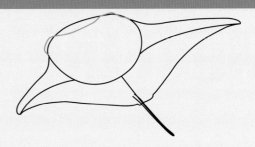

3 Next, draw the tail.

4 In this step, draw the head.

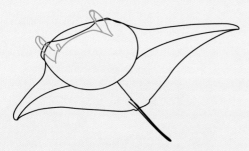

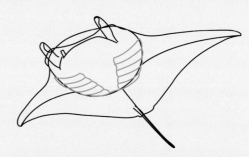

5 Now, draw the lobes and mouth.

6 Draw the gills, as shown.

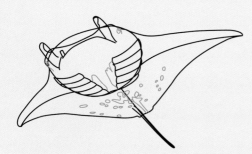

7 Draw the eyes and body spots.

8 Erase the extra lines and the stick figure frame.

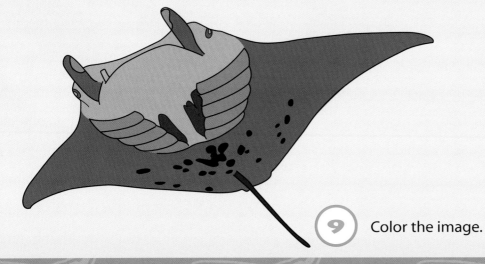

9 Color the image.

Meet the Octopus

The octopus is best known for its eight arms. Octopuses are shaped like a ball, with eight soft arms attached to one end. They live in oceans around the world.

Some octopuses can be very long. The giant Pacific octopus is the largest octopus in the world. The biggest giant Pacific octopus ever found had an arm span of about 30 feet (9 m). The smallest octopus lives in the Indian Ocean. It is the size of a dime.

Siphon

An octopus uses its soft body to swim. It squeezes water out of a tube called a siphon. Pushing water out of the siphon moves the octopus forward.

Arms
Octopuses use their arms for many tasks. They use their arms to eat and to **mate**. They also use them to build shelters. Octopuses can even open jars with the tips of their arms.

Suckers
Each of an octopus's arms has one or two rows of round **suckers**. The suckers help the octopus stick to rocks on the ocean floor. An octopus also uses its suckers to catch food. Octopuses eat a variety of small sea creatures, including shrimp and crabs.

Mouth
An octopus's mouth is on the bottom of its body. The mouth has a sharp beak. The octopus uses this beak to break open the hard shells of its food.

How to Draw an
Octopus

 Draw a stick figure of the octopus. Use ovals for the head and body, and curved lines for the arms.

2 Now, draw the head.

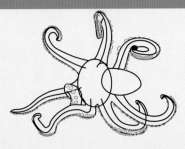

3 Next, draw the arms.

4 In this step, draw the suckers on the arms.

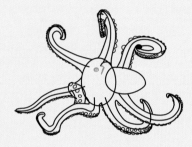

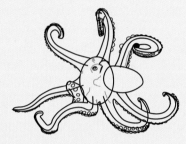

5 Next, draw the eye.

6 Now, draw small curved lines near the eye, as shown.

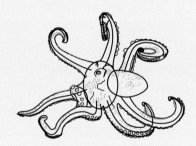

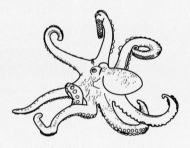

7 Add details to the head and arms.

8 Erase the extra lines and the stick figure frame.

9 Color the image.

Meet the Seahorse

The seahorse received its name because its head looks like a horse's head. A seahorse is a kind of fish. It has a long, slender body with a curled tail. There are about 35 kinds of seahorses. They live in **coral** reefs or **sea grass** near the ocean shore.

One of the smallest seahorses is the dwarf seahorse. It grows up to 2 inches (5 cm) long. One of the largest seahorses is the big-bellied seahorse. It is almost as long as a ruler.

Eyes
A seahorse can move each eye in a different direction. This helps it search larger areas for food.

Front Fins
Seahorses do not have ears. The flaps on the sides of their head are very small fins. They help steer the seahorse through water.

Mouth
The mouth of a seahorse is long and thin. The top and bottom jaws are joined to make a straw-like tube. Seahorses use this tube to suck up shrimp or other small animals that swim nearby.

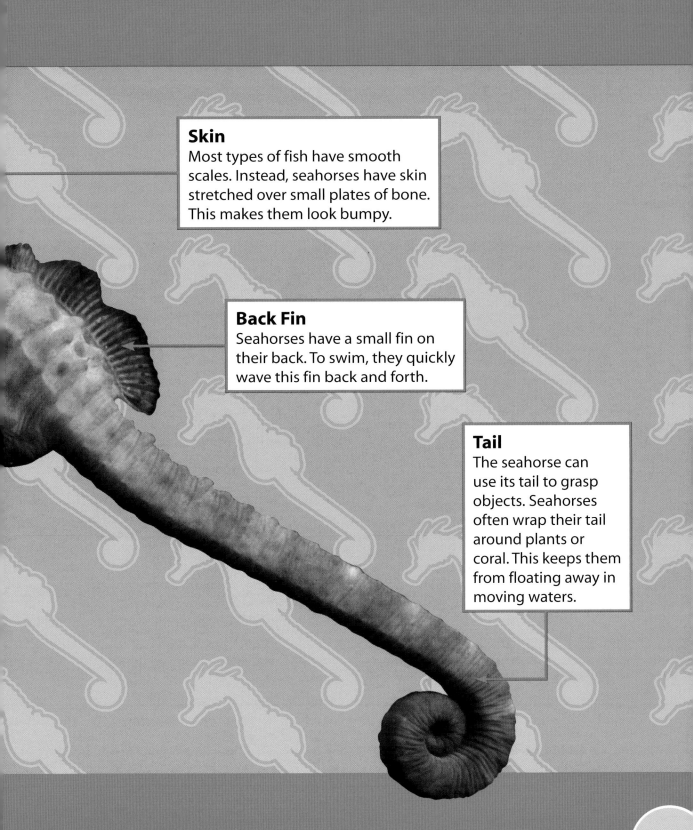

Skin
Most types of fish have smooth scales. Instead, seahorses have skin stretched over small plates of bone. This makes them look bumpy.

Back Fin
Seahorses have a small fin on their back. To swim, they quickly wave this fin back and forth.

Tail
The seahorse can use its tail to grasp objects. Seahorses often wrap their tail around plants or coral. This keeps them from floating away in moving waters.

How to Draw a
Seahorse

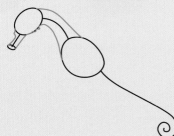

1 Start with a simple stick figure of the seahorse. Use ovals for the head and body, and lines for the tail and mouth.

2 Now, draw the trunk and mouth.

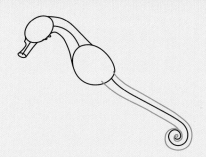

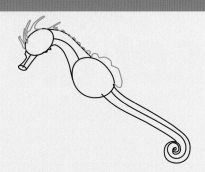

3 Draw the tail.

4 In this step, draw the back fin and the spikes on the head and trunk.

5 Next, draw the eye and gill opening.

6 Now, draw the plates on the body.

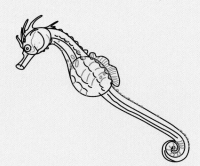

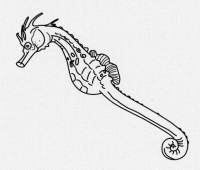

7 Add details to the body, tail, and back fin, as shown.

8 Erase the extra lines.

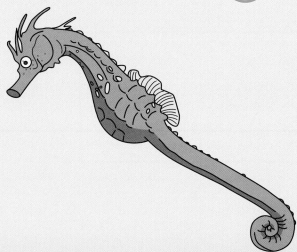

9 Color the image.

Meet the Sea Turtle

A sea turtle looks like a giant seashell with fins and a head. Sea turtles are **reptiles**, just like snakes and lizards. They live in the ocean, but they still need air to breathe.

There are seven types of sea turtle. The largest is the leatherback turtle. It can grow to 8 feet (2.4 m) long and weigh about 1,500 pounds (680 kilograms). The smallest type of sea turtle is the Kemp's ridley. It grows to 30 inches (76 cm).

Eyelids
A sea turtle has large upper eyelids. These eyelids protect the sea turtle's eyes.

Beak
Turtles are the only reptiles that do not have teeth. They use their strong, horn-like beak to crush their food. Sea turtles survive by eating a variety of underwater plants and animals, including fish, algae, and **crustaceans**.

Shell
Most sea turtles have shells. These shells are made up of hard sections called scutes. The shell protects the turtle's body. The leatherback turtle does not have a shell. Its body is protected by tough leathery skin.

Flippers
Sea turtles use their large, flat flippers to swim. The flippers help push sea turtles through water quickly. Some sea turtles can swim at speeds up to 20 miles (32 kilometers) per hour.

How to Draw a Sea Turtle

1. First, draw a stick figure of the turtle. Use ovals for the head and shell, and lines for the legs and flippers.

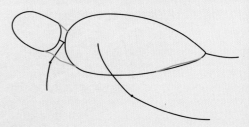

2. Now, draw the neck.

3 Draw the shell and beak.

4 In this step, draw the eye.

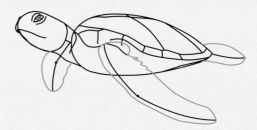

5 Next, draw the flippers and legs.

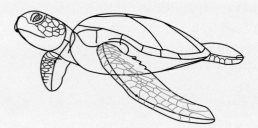

6 Draw the scales on the face, legs, and flipper.

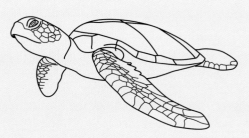

7 Add scales to the other flipper.

8 Erase the extra lines and the stick figure frame.

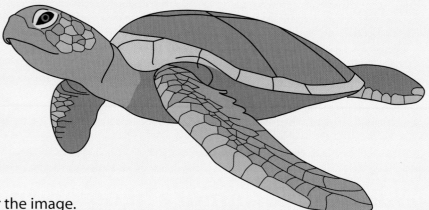

9 Color the image.

Test Your Knowledge of Underwater Life

1.

How many legs does a crab have?

Answer: 10

2.

What do jellyfish use their tentacles for?

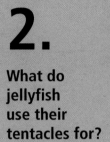

Answer: To catch food

3.

How many sets of fins does a manta ray have?

Answer: Two

4.

Where is an octopus's mouth located?

Answer: At the bottom of its body

5.

Why does a seahorse wrap its tail around coral?

Answer: To keep from floating away in moving waters

6.

What type of animal is a sea turtle?

Answer: A reptile

Want to learn more? Log on to av2books.com to access more content.

30

Draw an Environment

Materials
- Large white poster board
- Internet connection or library
- Pencils and crayons or markers
- Glue or tape

Steps
1. Complete one of the underwater life drawings in this book. Cut out the drawing.
2. Using this book, the internet, and a library, find out about your animal and the environment in which it lives.
3. Think about what might be found in this animal's environment. What does its environment look like? What sorts of plants or other objects are found near it? Are there other animals in its environment? What kinds of animals are these? What in your animal's environment is essential to its survival? What other important features might you find in this animal's environment?
4. On the large white poster board, draw an environment for your animal. Be sure to place all the features you noted in step 3.
5. Place the cutout animal in its environment with glue or tape. Color the animal's environment to complete the activity.

Glossary

adapted: changed to suit an environment

algae: green, slimy plant-like organisms without roots or leaves that develop in the ocean

antennae: long, thin body parts that extend from some animals' heads

communicaton: the sending and receiving of information

coral: a hard, stony substance that is made by a soft animal living in the ocean

crustaceans: a group of animals that have an hard outer shell, jointed legs, and a segmented body

imagination: the ability to form new creative ideas or images

mate: when a male and female come together to have young

reptiles: cold-blooded animals that are covered in scales and lay soft-shelled eggs on land

sea grass: a grass-like plant that grows on the ocean floor

suckers: rounded hollows that stick to surfaces

Log on to www.av2books.com

AV² by Weigl brings you media enhanced books that support active learning. Go to www.av2books.com, and enter the special code found on page 2 of this book. You will gain access to enriched and enhanced content that supplements and complements this book. Content includes video, audio, weblinks, quizzes, a slide show, and activities.

Audio
Listen to sections of the book read aloud.

Video
Watch informative video clips.

Embedded Weblinks
Gain additional information for research.

Try This!
Complete activities and hands-on experiments.

WHAT'S ONLINE?

Try This!	Embedded Weblinks	Video	EXTRA FEATURES
Complete an interactive drawing tutorial for each of the six underwater animals in the book.	Learn more about each of the six underwater animals in the book.	Watch a video about underwater animals.	**Audio** Listen to sections of the book read aloud.
			Key Words Study vocabulary, and complete a matching word activity.
			Slide Show View images and captions, and prepare a presentation
			Quizzes Test your knowledge.

AV² was built to bridge the gap between print and digital. We encourage you to tell us what you like and what you want to see in the future.
Sign up to be an AV² Ambassador at www.av2books.com/ambassador.

Due to the dynamic nature of the Internet, some of the URLs and activities provided as part of AV² by Weigl may have changed or ceased to exist. AV² by Weigl accepts no responsibility for any such changes. All media enhanced books are regularly monitored to update addresses and sites in a timely manner. Contact AV² by Weigl at 1-866-649-3445 or av2books@weigl.com with any questions, comments, or feedback.